Hello
SUMMER

A Fun Alphabet Adventure

This book belongs to:

A B C D E

F G H I J K

L M N O P

Q R S T U

V W X Y Z

Maze
Trace it!
1 2
Find it!
a l a m a s a o
b a f a l k a b
a a v b o a v a
3
1 2

HELLO
SUMMER

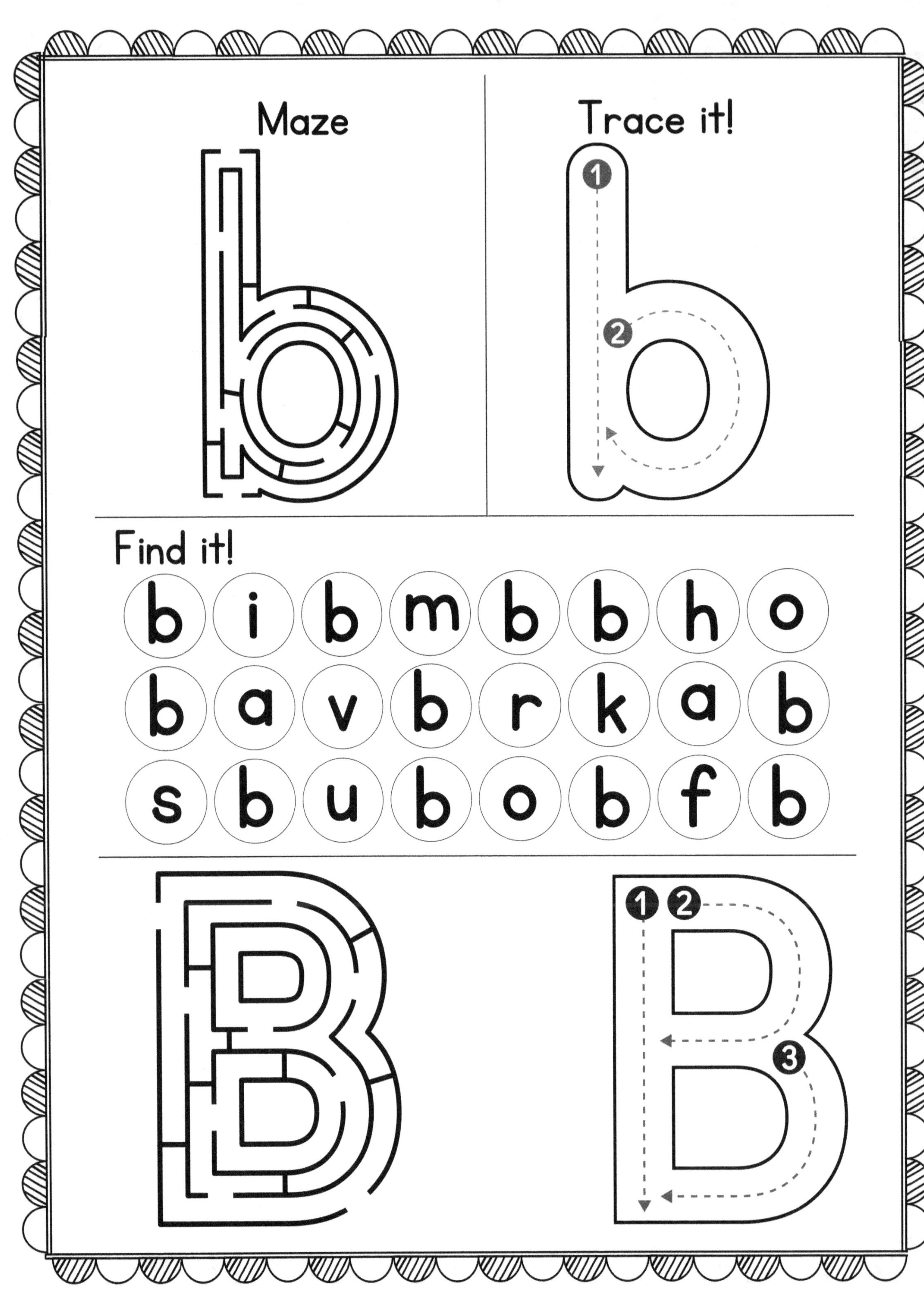

Maze
Trace it!
1
2
Find it!
b i b m b b h o
b a v b r k a b
s b u b o b f b
1 2
3

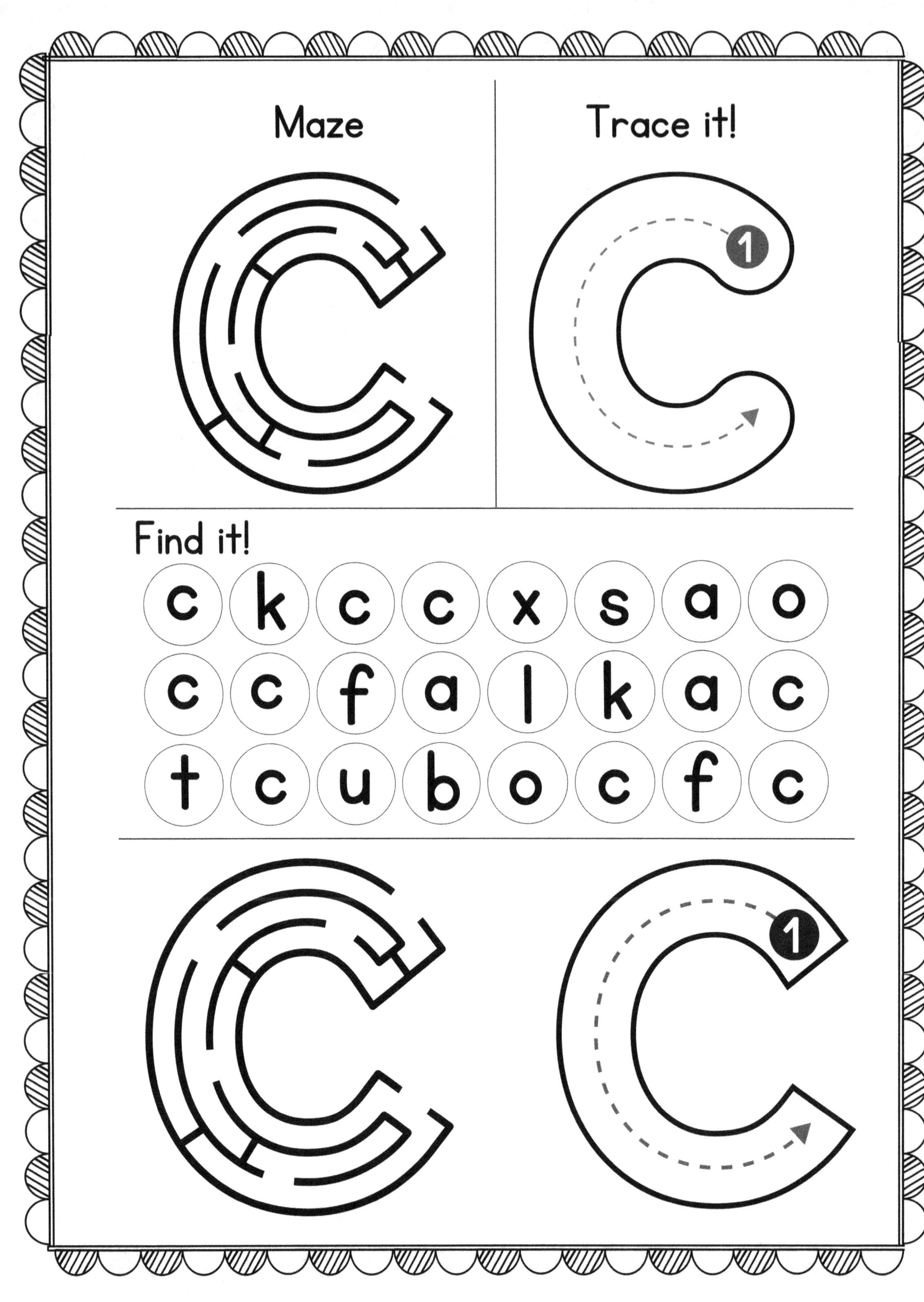

Maze
Trace it!
1
Find it!
c k c c x s a o
c c f a l k a c
t c u b o c f c
1

Maze

Trace it!

Find it!

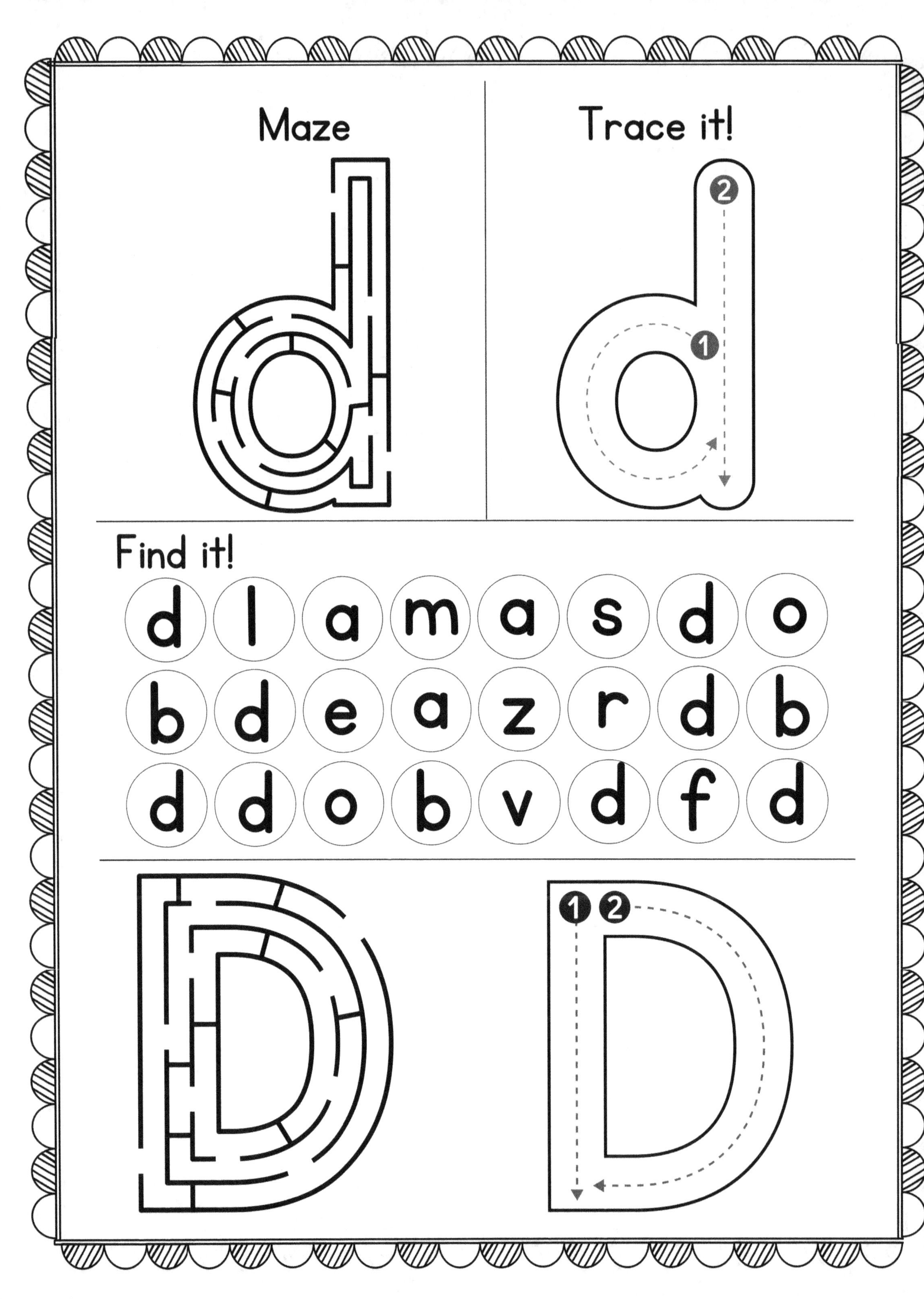

Maze

Trace it!

Find it!

e i e s e m v e

t e e a f k a b

e e v b o e f e

HELLO
SUMMER

Maze
Trace it!
1
2
Find it!
f l f m n s x o
b f f a f k d b
z f v b o u f f
1 2
3

Maze

Trace it!

Find it!

g h e s g m v g
t g g a g k g t
h g g b o w z g

Summer
LOVE
ICE CREAM

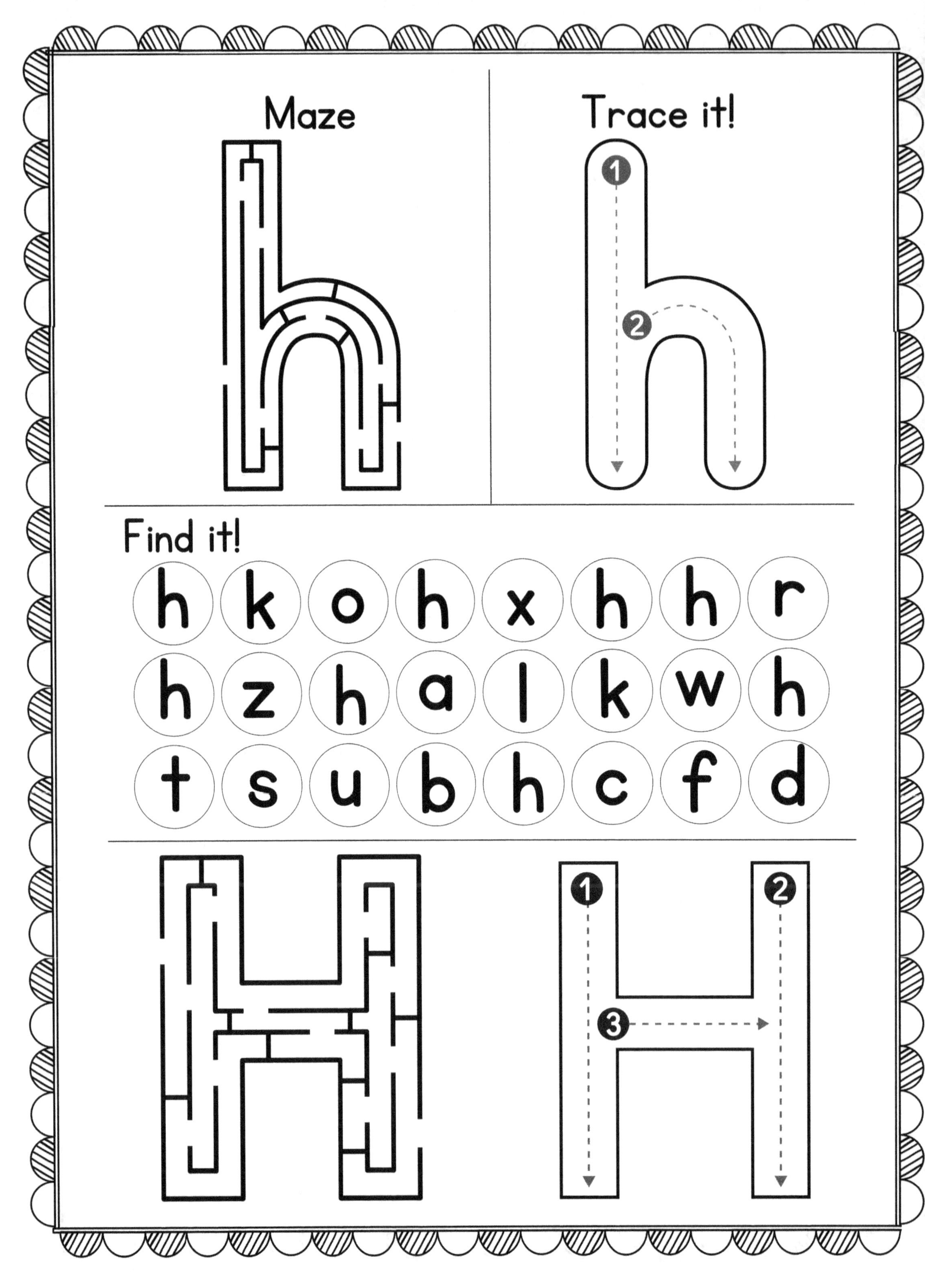
Maze
Trace it!
1
2
Find it!
h k o h x h h r
h z h a l k w h
t s u b h c f d
1 2
3

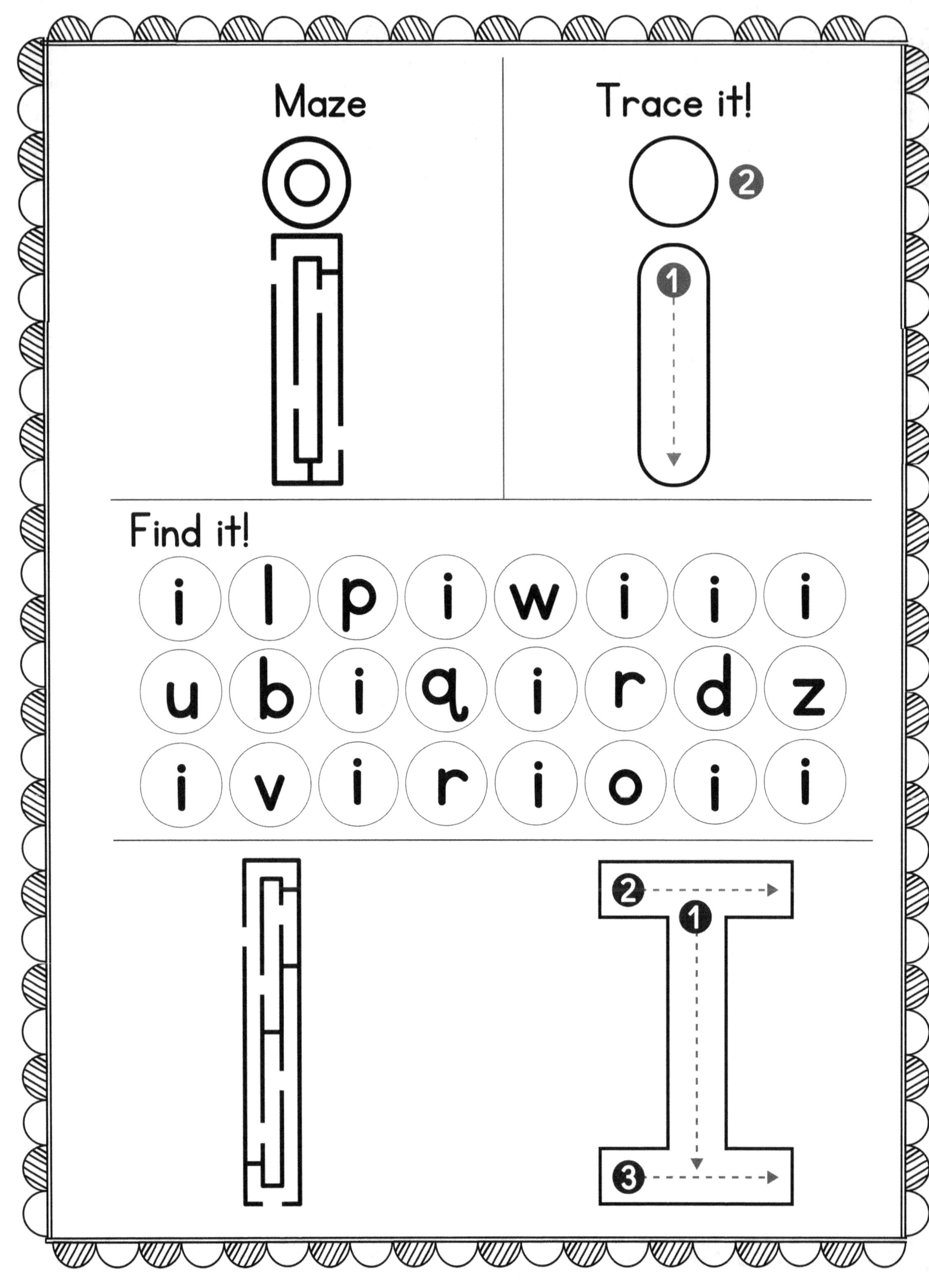
Maze
Trace it!
2
1
Find it!
i l p i w i i i
u b i q i r d z
i v i r i o i i
2
1
3

SUMMER

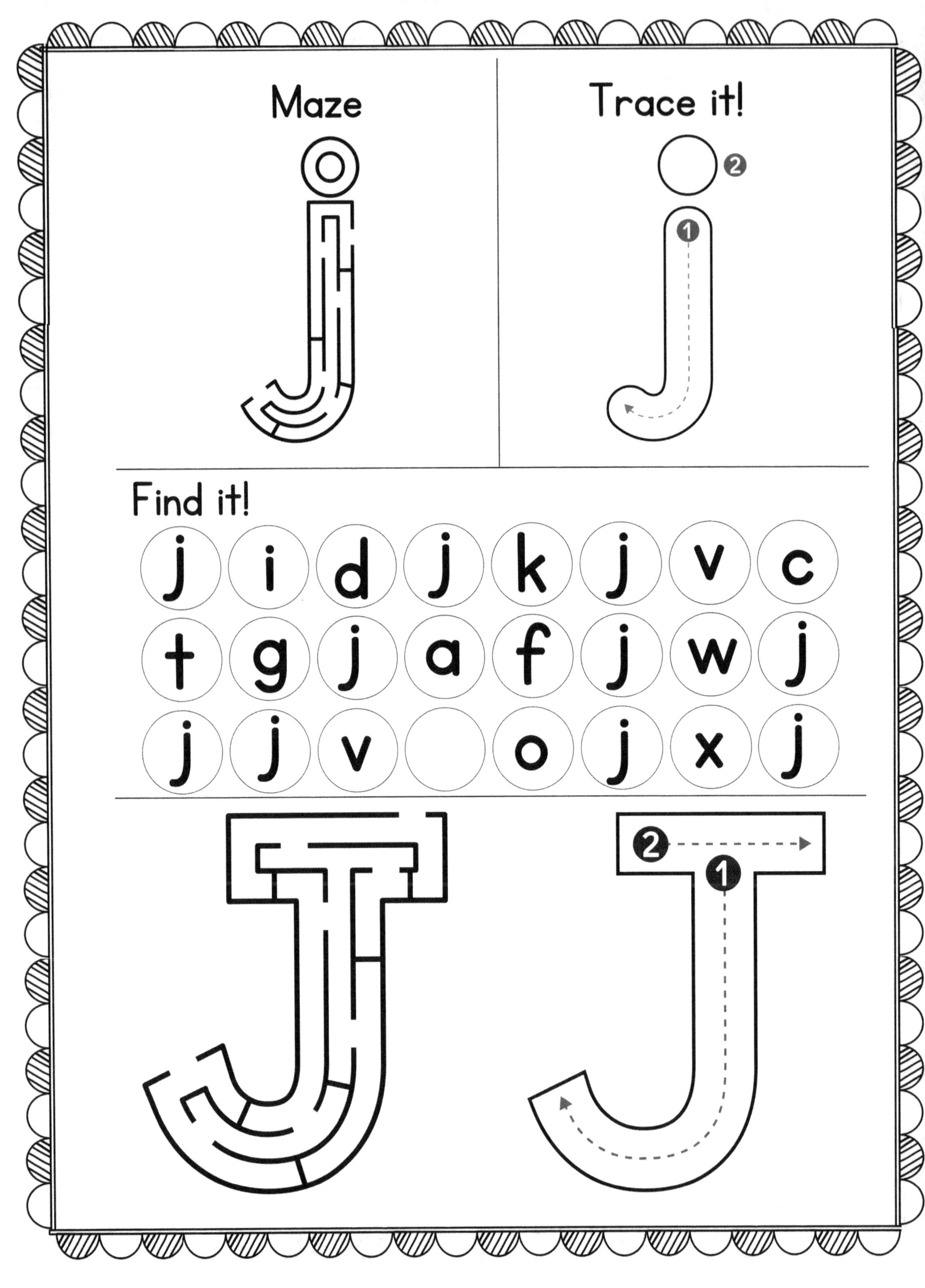

Maze
Trace it!
Find it!
j i d j k j v c
t g j a f j w j
j j v o j x j

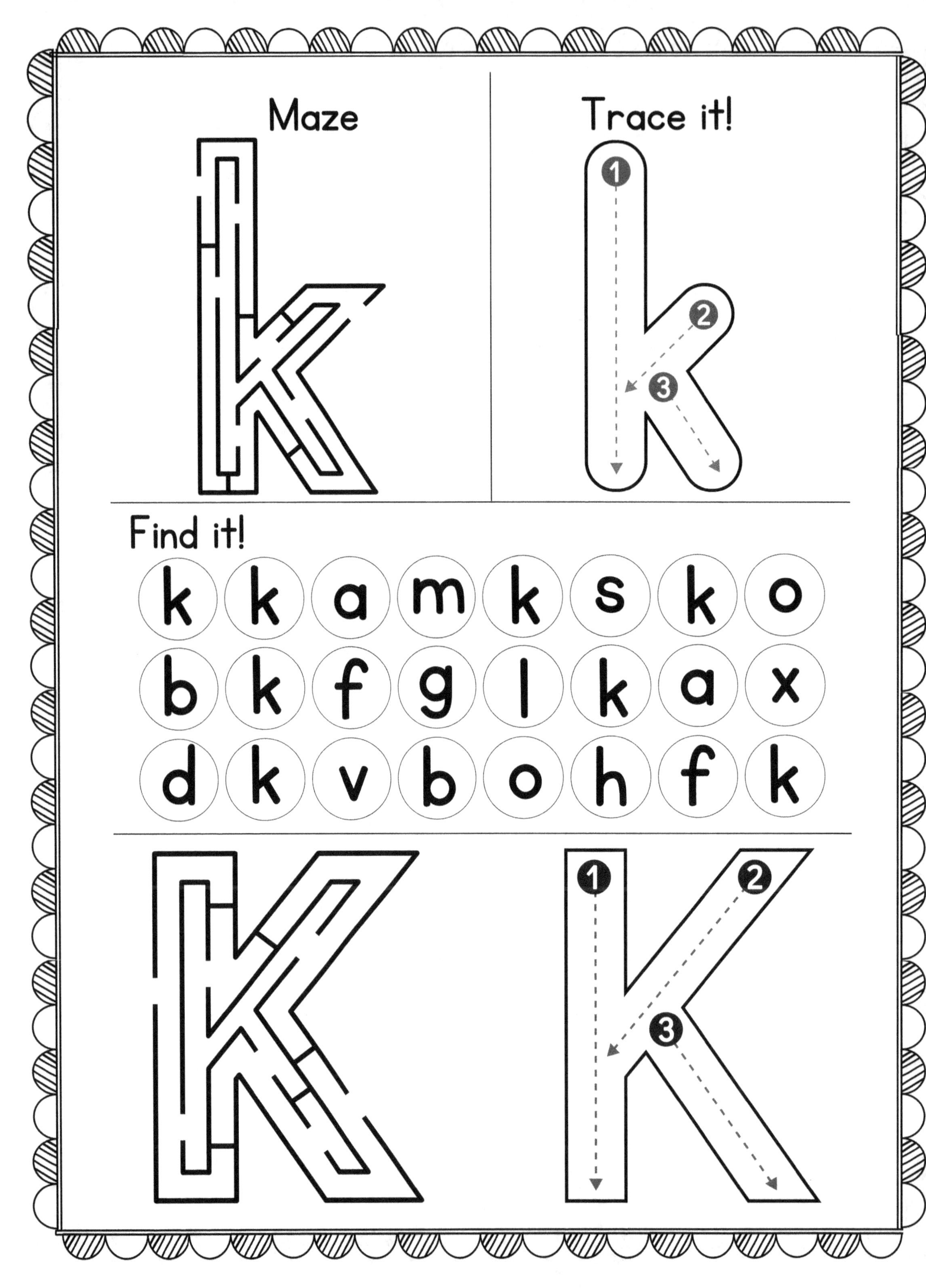

Maze
Trace it!
1
2
3
Find it!
k k a m k s k o
b k f g l k a x
d k v b o h f k
1
2
3

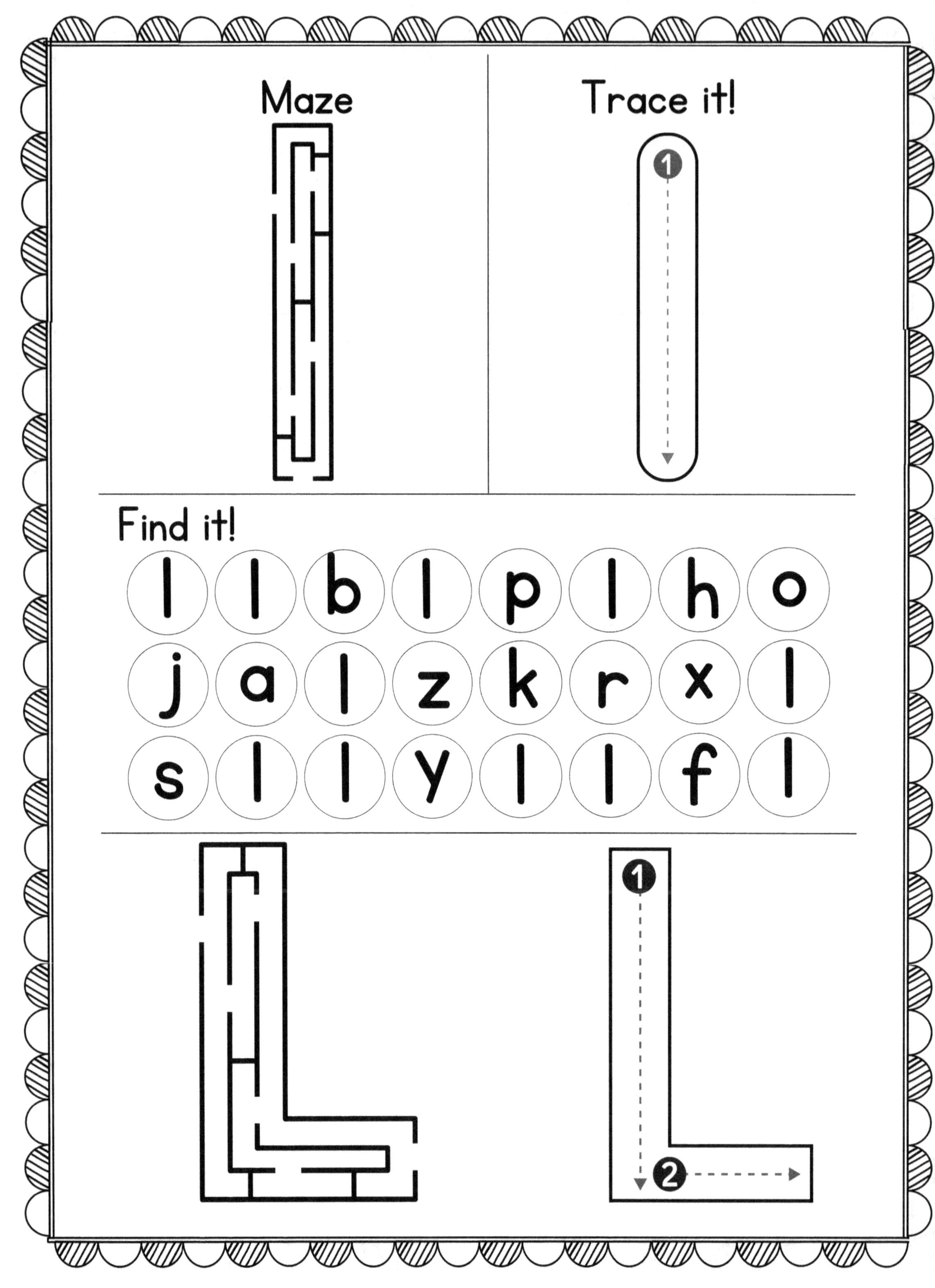

Maze

Trace it!

Find it!

M m M m M m M m

M

m

M

m

M

m

M m M m M m M m

Maze

Trace it!

Find it!

m	x	w	m	x	s	g	m
m	q	m	a	m	k	i	m
m	z	m	b	o	c	f	m

M m M m M m M m

M

m

M

m

M

m

M m M m M m M m

N n N n N n N n N n

N

n

N

n

N

n

N n N n N n N n N n

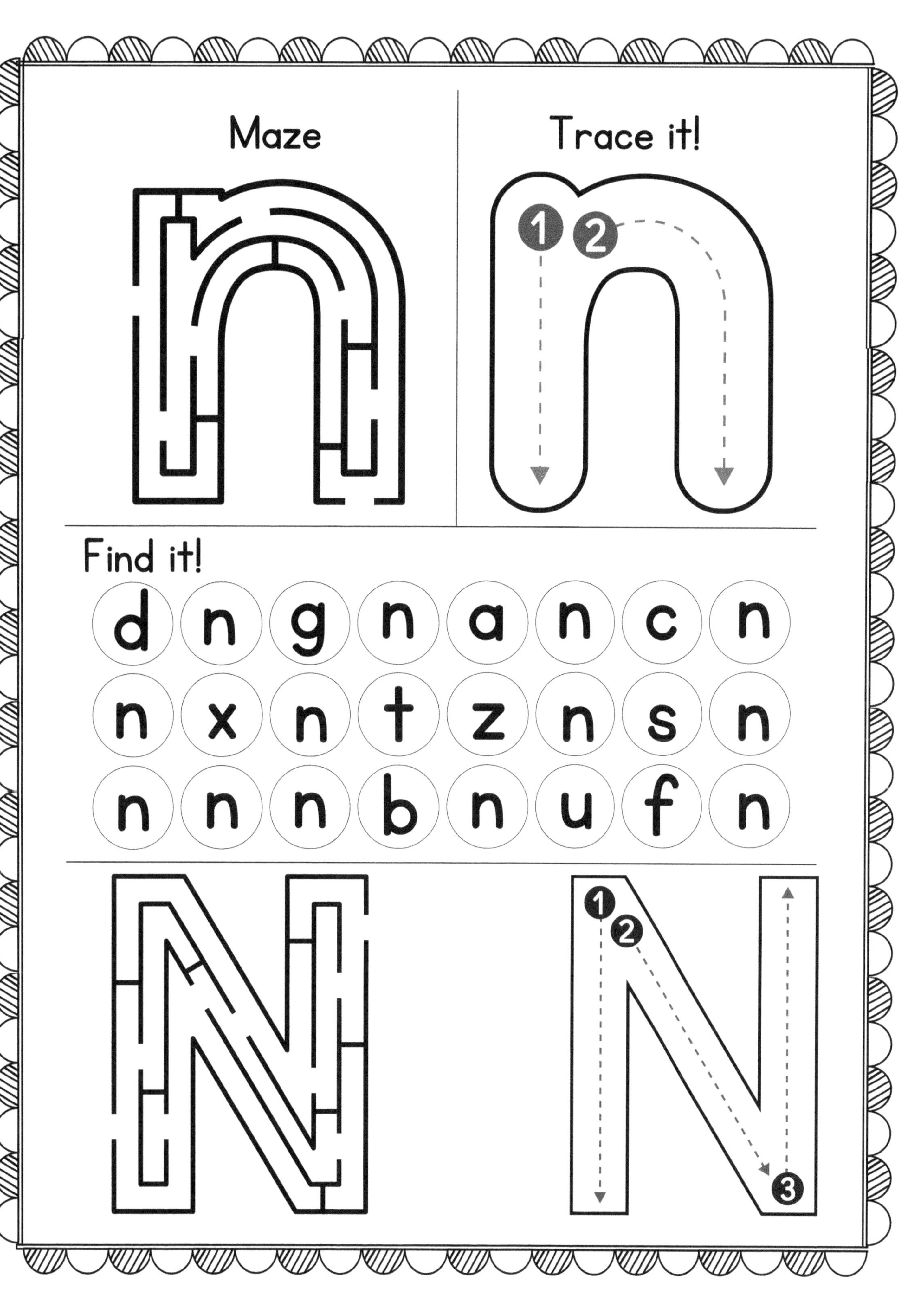

Maze
Trace it!
1 2
Find it!
d n g n a n c n
n x n t z n s n
n n n b n u f n
1 2
3

Maze

Trace it!

Find it!

o i g o k m v o

o e o j o o a o

s o v b o n f u

Maze

Trace it!

Find it!

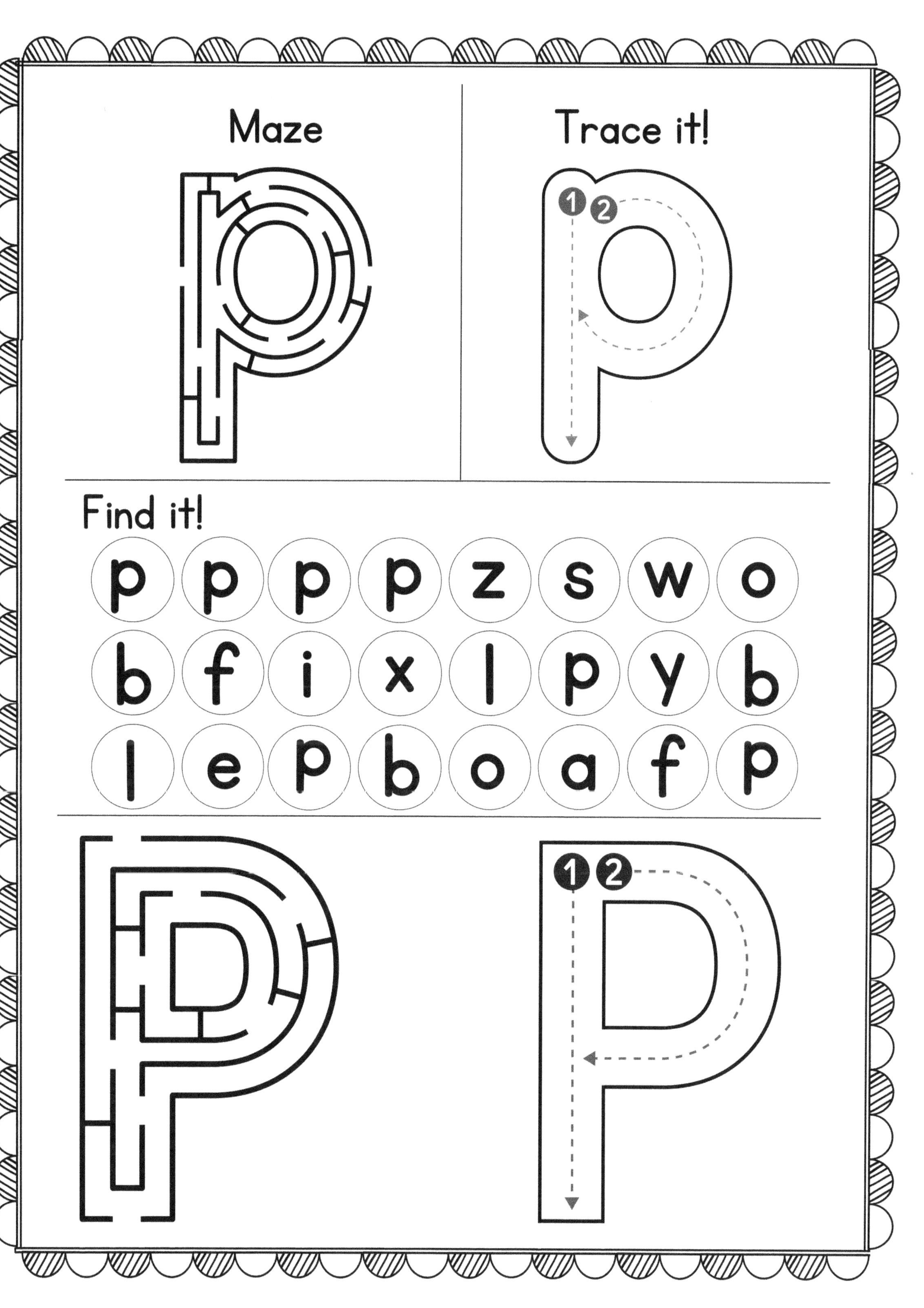

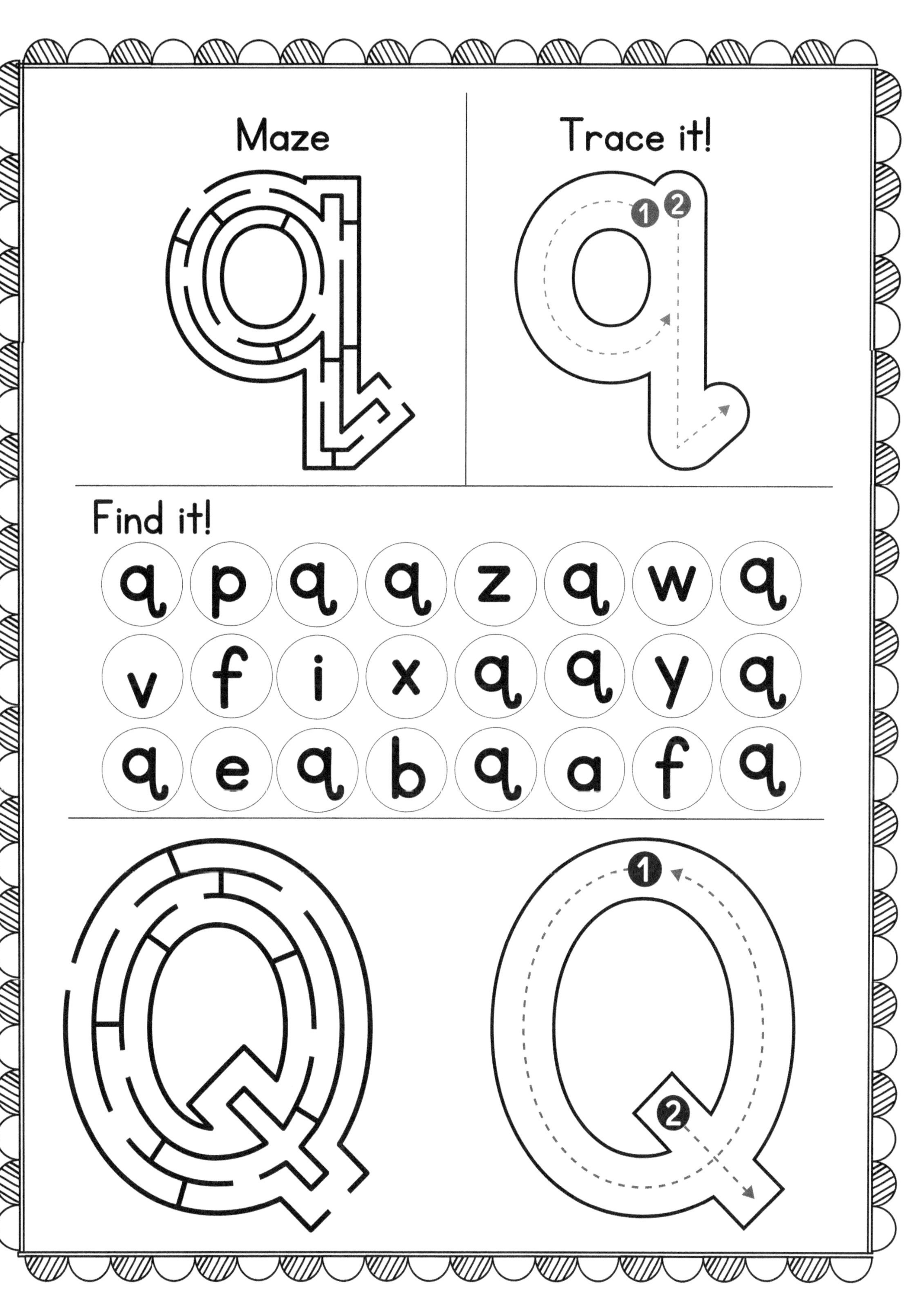

Maze
Trace it!
1 2
Find it!
q p q q z q w q
v f i x q q y q
q e q b q a f q
1
2

R r R r R r R r R r
R
r
R
r
R
r
R r R r R r R r R r

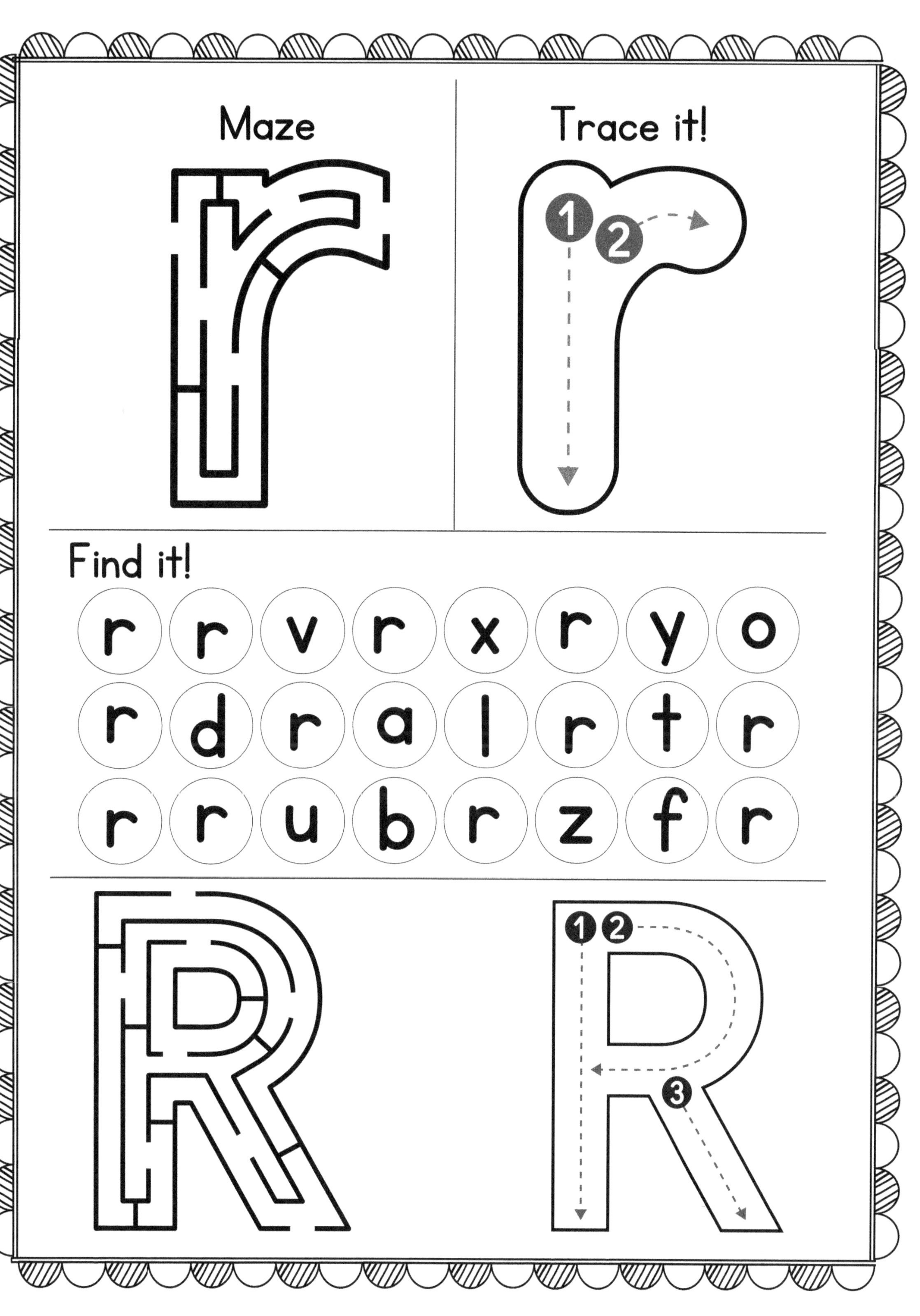
Maze
Trace it!
Find it!
r r v r x r y o
r d r a l r t r
r r u b r z f r
1 2
1 2
3

R r R r R r R r R r
R
r
R
r
R
r
R r R r R r R r R r

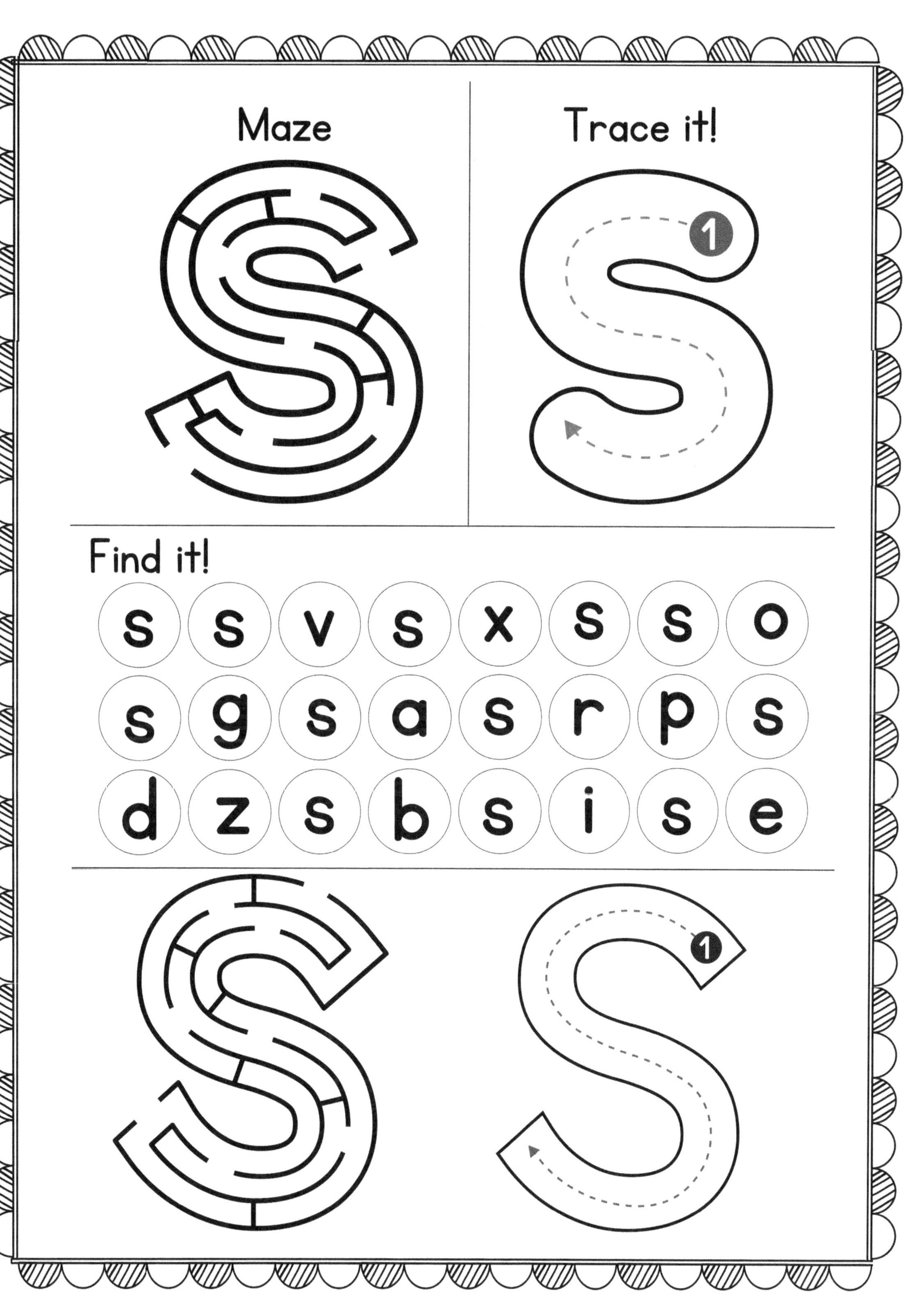

Maze

Trace it!

Find it!

s	s	v	s	x	s	s	o
s	g	s	a	s	r	p	s
d	z	s	b	s	i	s	e

SUMMER

Maze

Trace it!

Find it!

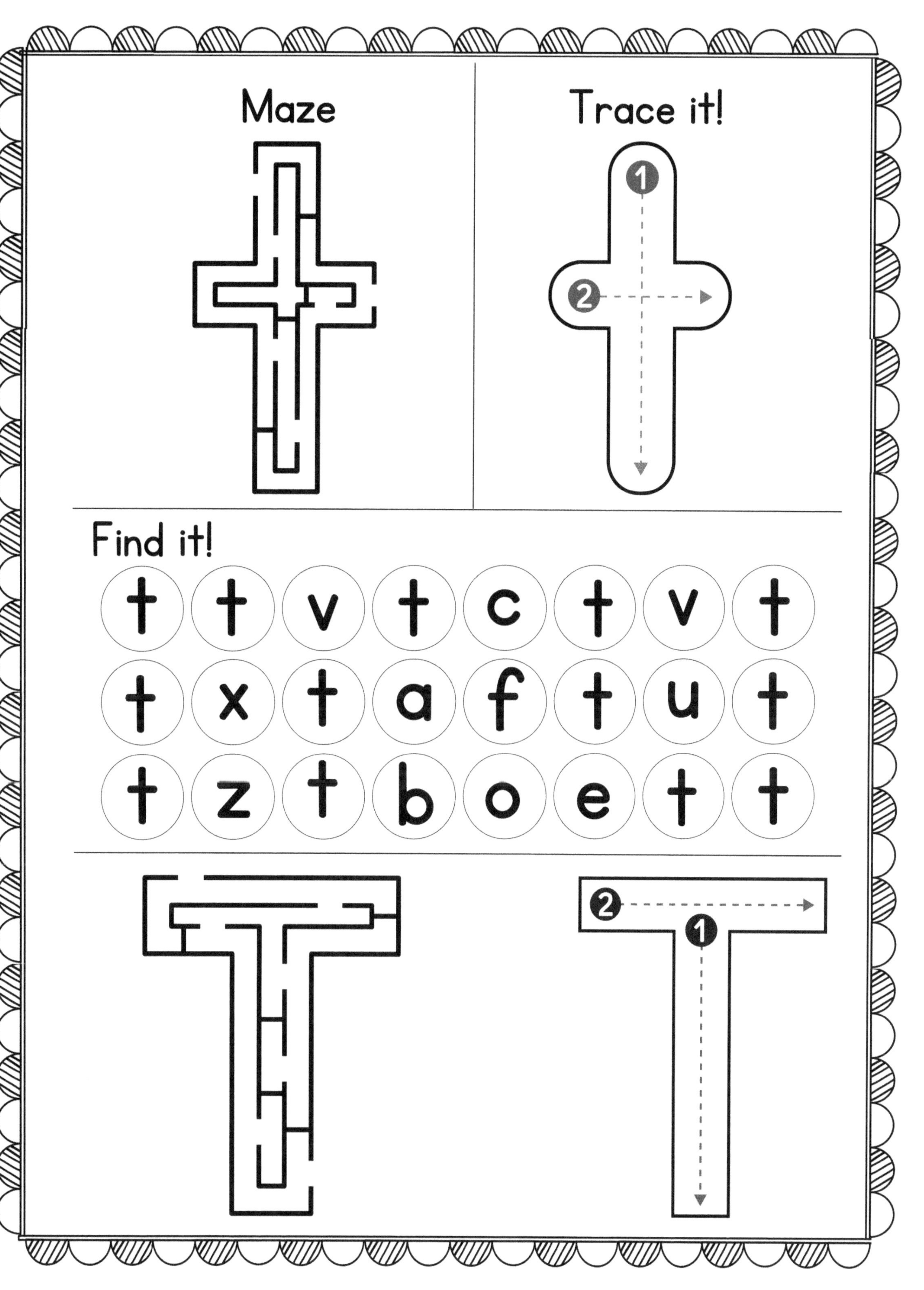

Maze

Trace it!

Find it!

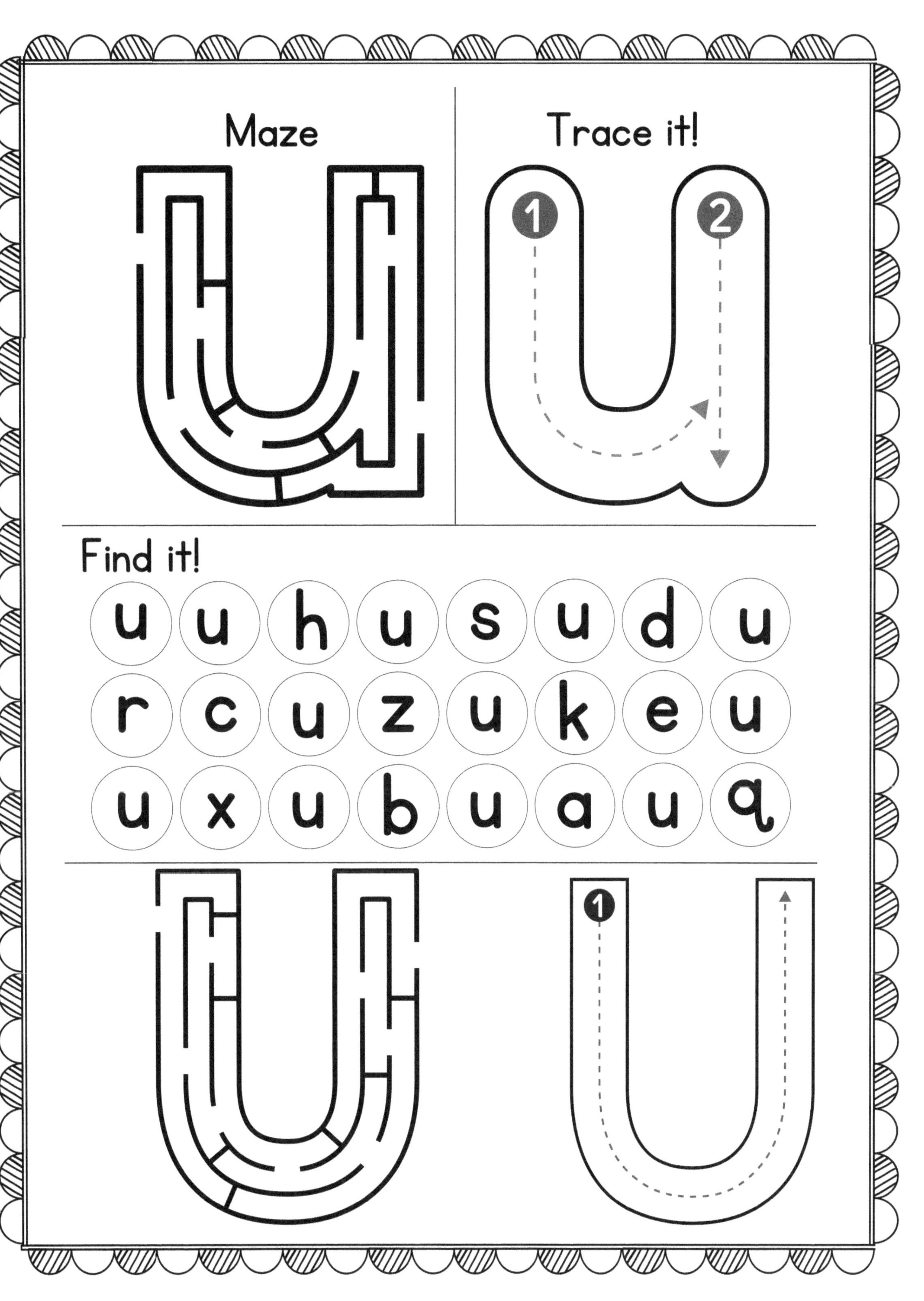

Maze
Trace it!
1
2
Find it!
e   v   i   v   j   v   h   v
s   r   v   d   v   v   a   v
v   g   v   t   v   b   v   v
1
2

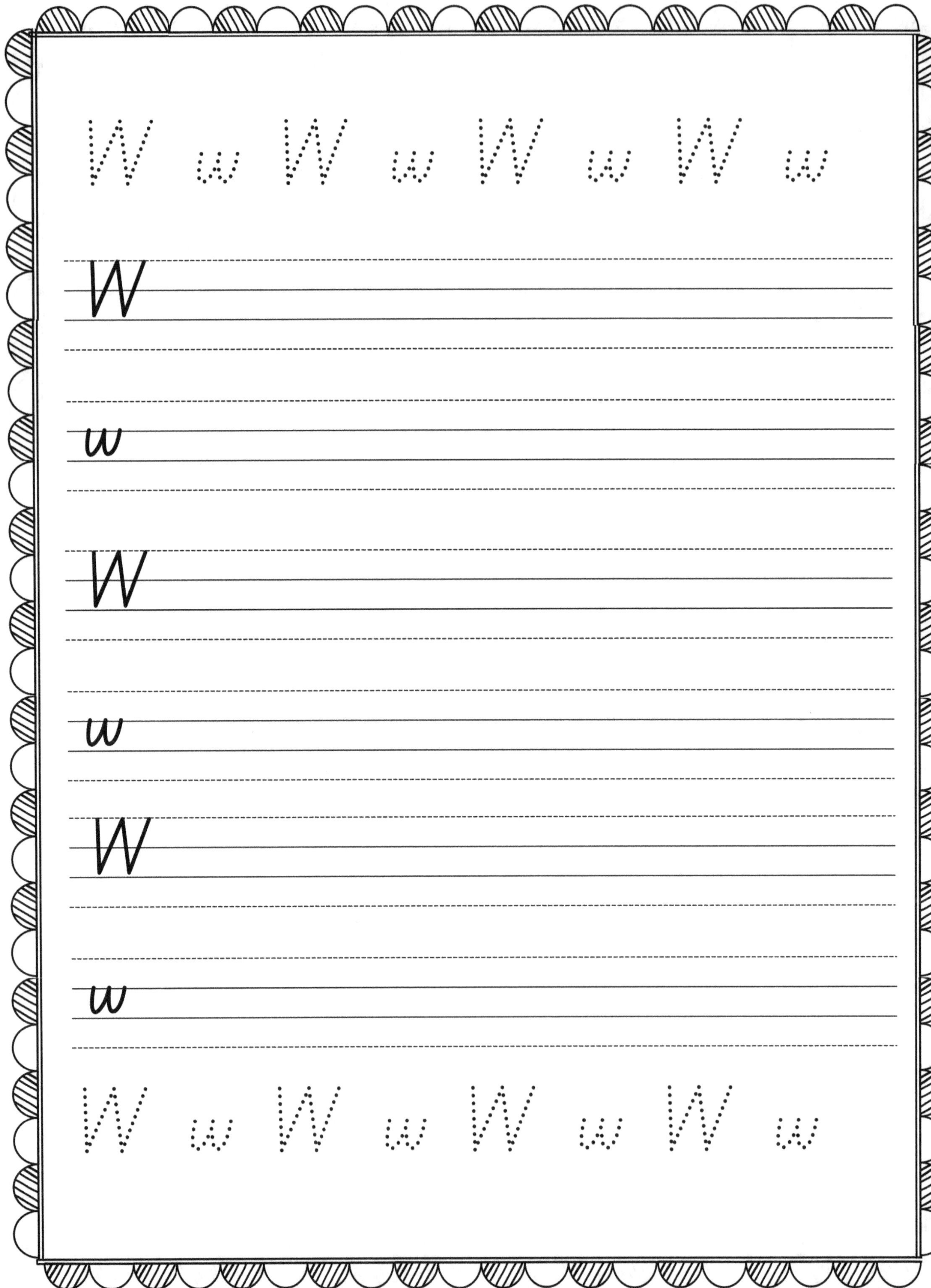

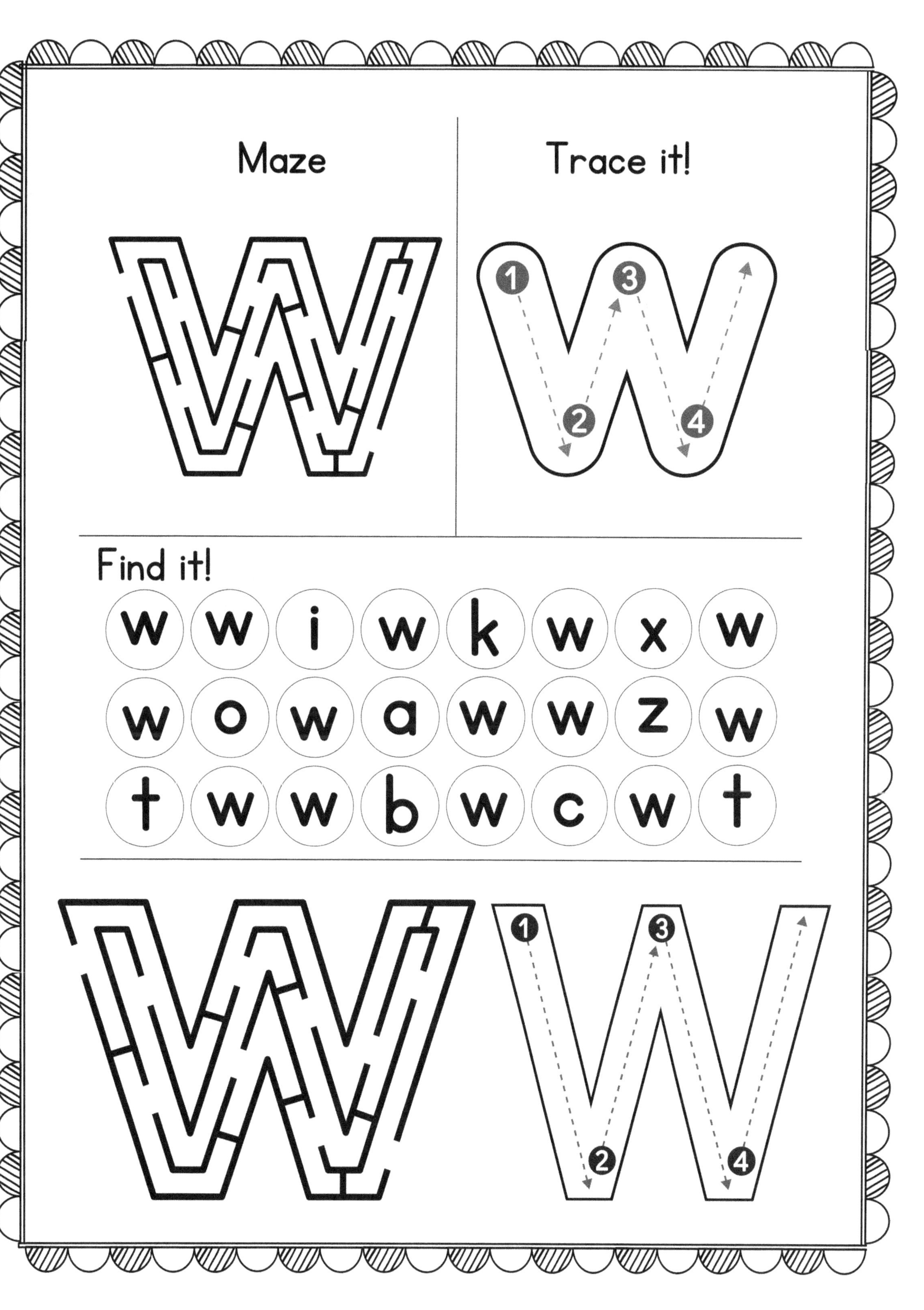

Maze
Trace it!
1
3
2
4
Find it!
w w i w k w x w
w o w a w w z w
t w w b w c w t
1
3
2
4

SUMMER
FUN

Maze

Trace it!

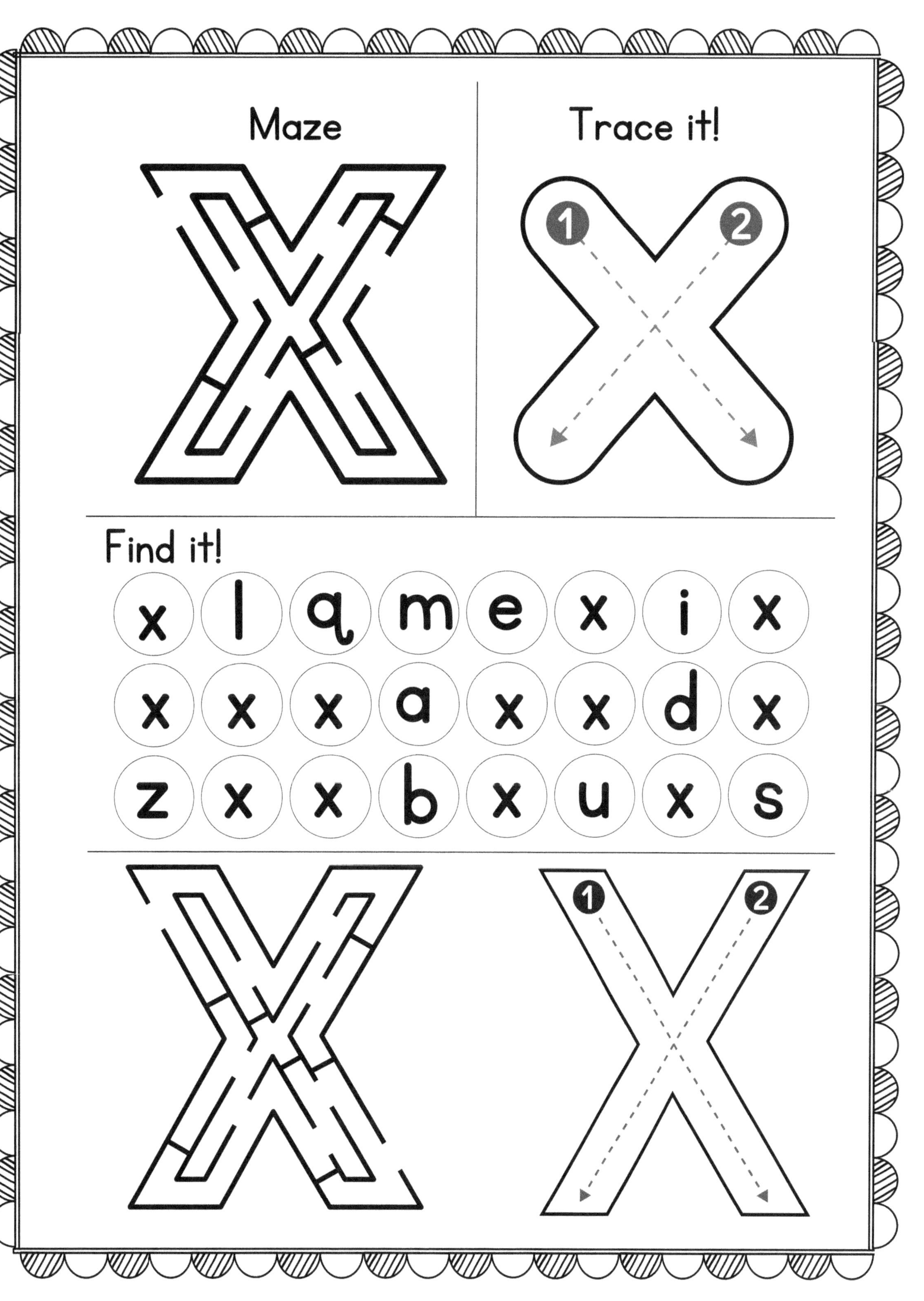

Find it!

x	l	q	m	e	x	i	x
x	x	x	a	x	x	d	x
z	x	x	b	x	u	x	s

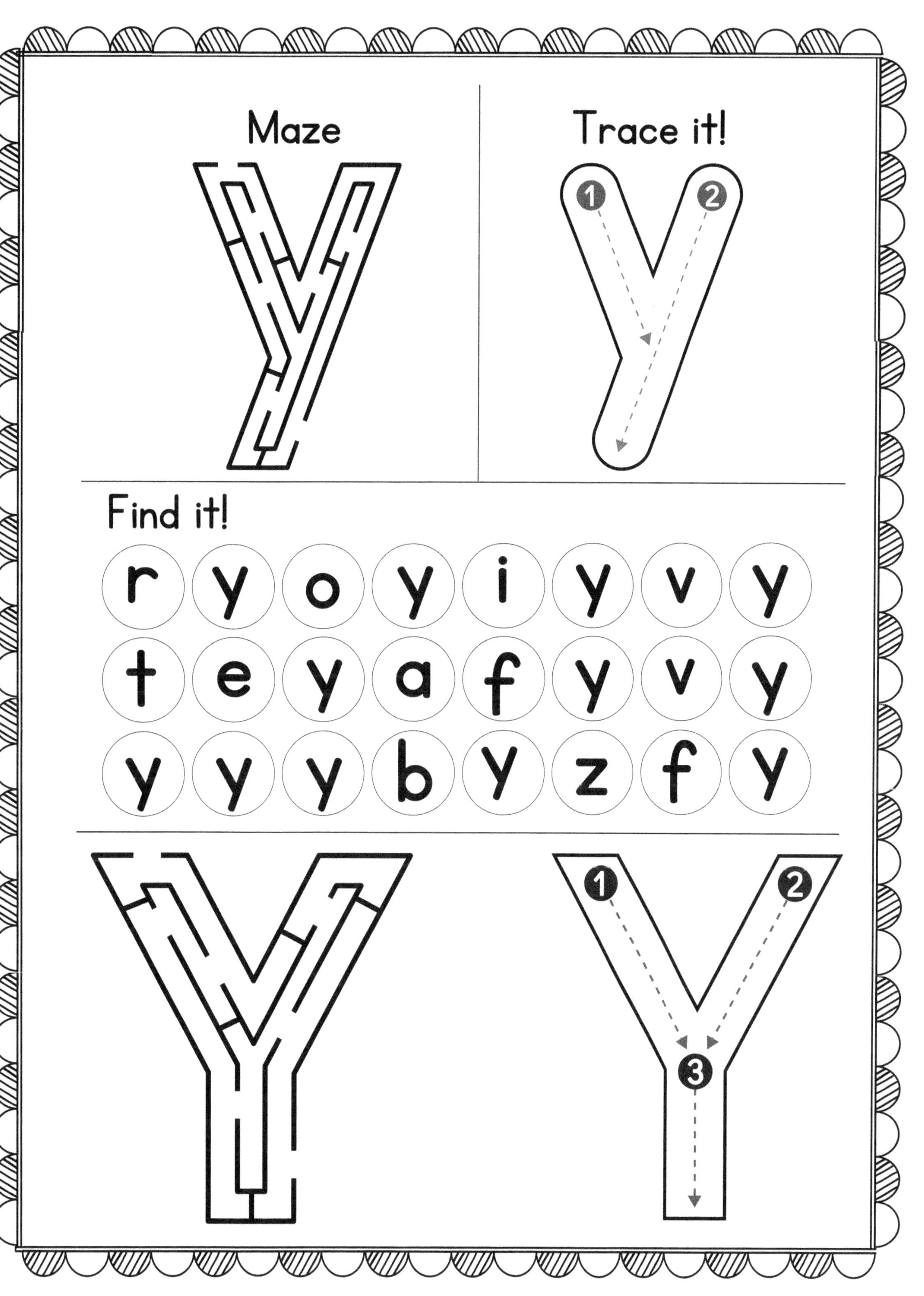
Maze
Trace it!
1
2
Find it!
r y o y i y v y
t e y a f y v y
y y y b y z f y
1
2
3

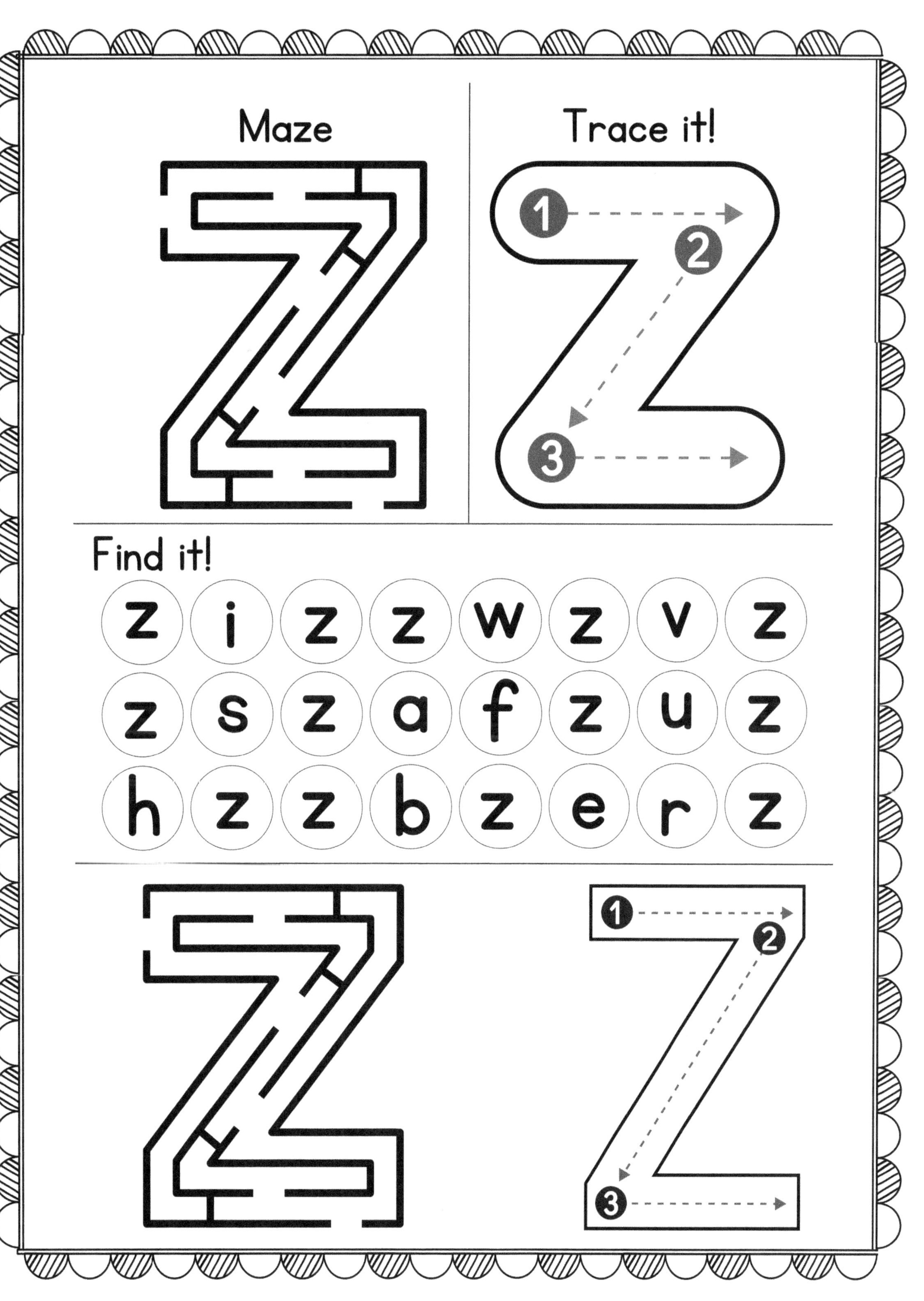

Maze
Trace it!
1
2
3
Find it!
z i z z w z v z
z s z a f z u z
h z z b z e r z
1
2
3

I
LOVE
SUMMER

SUMMER
FUN!

www.ingramcontent.com/pod-product-compliance
Lightning Source LLC
LaVergne TN
LVHW060339200726
843506LV00008B/555